The Space Between Our Danger and Delight

Dan Vera

BEOTHUK BOOKS
2009

The type is Cheltenham with titling in Eagle Light.

Published by
BEOTHUK BOOKS
3323 14th Street NE
Washington, DC 20017
www.beothukbooks.com

No part of this book may be reproduced without
written permission of the author and publisher.

© 2009 by Dan Vera
All rights reserved
Manufactured in the United States of America.
First Edition.

Library of Congress Cataloging-in-Publication Data

Vera, Dan
The Space Between Our Danger and Delight: poems /
by Dan Vera — 1st ed.

ISBN 978-0-615-25371-8

ACKNOWLEDGMENTS

The Amistad: "Goldrush of Comparisons"
BARK!: "Translating the Family Feud," "Explaining the Poem"
Beltway Poetry Quarterly: "Constellations of Delight," "DC to Newark/Astral Woman," "Father's Day For Gay Boys," "Poem of Delight," "Sterling on 12th Street,"
"We Abide In The Irony," "Winter Solstice Meditation"
Delaware Poetry Review: "Beautiful Pesach Moon,"
"Emily Dickinson at the Poetry Slam"
Dog Blessings: "The Nature of His Knowing"
Konch: "Gerald Early Can't See Latinos"

For Peter

CONTENTS

ONE
Benares   11
Poem of Delight   12
DC To Newark/Astral Woman   13
Emily Dickinson at the Poetry Slam   14
Beautiful Pesach Moon   16
Chicory   17
Stone Dead Keep Watch   18
Quarter Head Shrinkage   19
We Abide In The Irony   20
Winter Solstice Meditation   21
A Trace of Us   22
The Last Word of the Day is Love   23

TWO
Crickets & Yellow Dogs   27
Sleight of Hand Chicken Soup   29
The Sugars of Kindness   30
English As A Second Irritating Language   32
For Joel Who Held The Word For Me   33
Father's Day for Gay Boys   34
Fe Esperanza y Caridad   35
I Have No Poems For You Now Texas   36

THREE
While the Audience Waits for the Poet to Finish
Explaining the Poem He Has Yet To Read   39
Gerald Early Can't See Latinos   40
Translating the Family Feud   41
Spitzer Linked to a Prostitution Ring   42
Celibacy   43
For Some Executors of Gay Writers   44
On the Removal of Red   45

FOUR
The Cold Rush of Comparisons   49
We Learn How Creed Crows   50
The Nature Of His Knowing   51
Constellations of Delight   52
In Which the Poet Savors the Chicken Soup
Brought to Him At the Very Hour of His Need   53
Ode to the Black Nationalist Pharaoh Head
of Georgia Avenue   54
Sterling On 12th Street   55

ONE

Benares

To pass among them or touch any one, or rest my arm ever so lightly
round his or her neck for a moment, what is this then?
I do not ask any more delight, I swim in it as in a sea.   Walt Whitman

My hand through tall grasses,
you breathe soft
then hard,
as I lie here,
in the bed I once dreamed of,
while birds sing their own songs outside the window
and the dog lies sleeping in his own dreams.

What do pilgrims do
when they finally reach the river?
They bathe in it.
They do not question the tides.
They do not taste the brine.
They bathe in it as in a sea.

Poem of Delight

What are the chemical properties of delight?
What physical law rules delight?
In which commandment did the Hebrew God command delight?
Does delight ever go on sale?
Does delight ever go on vacation?
What is the temperature of delight?
Who came first: the delighted chicken or the delighted egg?
What are the elemental principles of delight?

If I dropped delight from the Empire State Building at exactly the same time you dropped delight from the second story window of your apartment, which delight would land first?

If day follows night, does this mean delight follows delight?
With a billion sparkling beings illuminating the sky,
Is midnight the time of shimmering delight?
And if I feel delight at the twinkling of stars that long burned out in the blue ovens of night, What is the half-life of delight?

An East-bound train from Omaha to Denver is traveling at 110 miles an hour and a West-bound train from Denver to Omaha is traveling at 95 miles an hour. They both leave their respective stations at the same time and the distance between Denver and Omaha is 537 miles. How much time will it take the train conductors to feel delight at their meeting?

Is depression jealous of delight?
Do the bells at the top of the hill ring with anything but delight?

I was walking through the aisles of the grocery store when I stumbled upon a pyramid display of delight. I placed one in my basket and proceeded to the checkout line. But when the cashier tried to scan it, he couldn't find a universal price code for delight.

    "Price check on Aisle 3!"

Love is just the space between our danger and delight.

DC to Newark/Astral Woman

I sat next to a woman on a plane
who astral projected her body
right out of her seat,
by my face,
and through the tiny window at my ear.

We were flying beside the Atlantic
and she only wanted to dip her astral-projected toe
in the saltwater.

I saw her blue form flash through the air
hurtling towards the water.
She splashed her foot up to her knee
and just stood there in mid air,
a big soothing astral projected smile
crossing her wide blue face.

Just as quickly
she zipped through the air like a blue bottle rocket
through the window
past my face
and into her seat.

"Pepsi. Diet Pepsi. 7 UP?" the passing steward asked.
"Pepsi please" the woman responded.

She took a long drink
turned to me and said,
"Parched."

Emily Dickinson at the Poetry Slam

I will tell you why she rarely ventured from her house.
It happened like this:

One day she took the train to Boston,
made her way to the darkened room,
put her name down in cursive script
and waited her turn.

Poets before her stood and rhymed,
followed a meter tight and expected,
outdoing one another in a monotonous clip.

When they read her name aloud
she made her way to the stage
straightened the papers in her hands –
pages and envelopes, the backs of grocery bills,
she closed her eyes for a minute,
took a breath,
and began.

From her mouth perfect words exploded,
intact formulas of light and darkness.
She dared to rhyme with words like cochineal
and described the skies like diadem.
Obscurely worded incantations filled the room
with an alchemy that made the very molecules quake.

The solitary words she handled
in her upstairs room with keen precision
came rumbling out to make the electric lights flicker.

40 members of the audience
were treated for hypertension.
20 year old dark haired beauties found their heads
had turned a Moses White.

Her second poem erased the memory of every cell phone
in the nightclub,
and by the fourth line of the sixth verse
the grandmother in the upstairs apartment
had been cured of her rheumatism.

The papers reported the power outages.
The area hospitals taxed their emergency generators
and sirens were heard to wail through the night.

Quietly she made her way to the exit,
walked to the terminal and rode back to Amherst.

She never left her room again
and never read such syllables aloud.

Beautiful Pesach Moon

And I who am not Jewish,
am befriended this night,
made warm by strangers,
fed at a common table,
allowed to trip my tongue
pronouncing millennial old
sacred prayers over the bitter
  and the sweet.

And now returning home,
the moon,
like a plate awaiting charoset,
like matzoh floating in the bluest soup of sky,
shines her brightest lamp down on me.

And like this night's Haggadah
I am made to connect the old with the new.
So as the plague of frogs reminded us
  of an ecology without frogs,
the Military Drive I ride upon
reminds me of the pestilence
of this misbegotten war we are in.

This moon too shines over Baghdad,
casting her light over the bitter and the bittersweet.

Chicory

Resilient blue glitter of the empty yard!

Tiny lapis wonder,
sheltered under Queen Anne's umbrellas,
your consort in swelter.

I cannot hold you Chicory,
miraculous azure bird which stands cool in heat
and wilts when cut for the inside room.

Oh Chicory!
Blue paper hat of late summer!

Your names are your own poetry,
Blue sailor.
Coffee weed.
Bitter leaf.

Precious fleeting hearty flower,
when other blossoms surrender and fade
under the blinding brow of August imperial heat,
you persist,
the ever rebellious blue passion of summer.

Stone Dead Keep Watch

Today the statues stand lifeless and longing.

Although he is offered the sword each day, L'Enfant
never takes it from the maiden beneath him.

And the men beneath Von Steuben gaze
an eternity in each other's marble eyes.
"Take the sword from my hand, my master."
"Give me the blade, my runner, my soldier boy."

Beneath them the tourists of July trade glances
with the hunger strikers and the Buddhist nun
who beats her tiny drum for peace.

They do not look up at the men in their fancy coats
with their forgotten names and achievements.
They do not know them beyond L'Enfant's desolate metro
stop.

Mutely the pedestalled dead look down on the unarmed
who take pictures of a White House at war
while rooftop sharp shooters stare out at them
and the paneled vans stand idling
on the sidewalks of the silent park.

Quarter Head Shrinkage

Your head is getting smaller on the coin George.

In '67 your noggin was large and long
and jutting into LIBERTY.

By '86 you were round-faced,
more Charlie Brown than
father of the country.

Now in the new millennium
you are downright Roman small,
more waves in your powdered 'do,
with a neck too large for that pretty head of yours.

How they shrink you General.
By 2050 I suppose
You'll be nothing but the rattail of your wig.

A sad reminder of your famed humility.
But a boon to anyone wagering tails.

We Abide In The Irony

We gloried for hours in seventeenth century masterworks,
deep in subterranean rooms of Sackler Gallery,
Hokusai's Japanese ukiyo-e art.

Every fold of fabric painted precise,
chrysanthemum, crane and willow tree,
cases filled with the steady hand of
four hundred year old genius.

We arose to Spring Washington
in a full blossomed Saturday,
walked to the Roosevelt memorial.

Four administrations,
four rooms of frieze and fixed type salutes
to civil liberty in granite.
Beloved monument to the interner of the
descendents of Japanese ukiyo-e artists.

At the end of the 2nd World War,
we retired to the reflecting pool,
walked beneath the pink colored branches of
a long ago emperor's shame-faced gift.

Felt the silk fabric of history folding and enfolding again.

Winter Solstice Meditation

This cold morning everything struggles with the cold.
Even the honey requires extra effort to extract it from the jar.
This cold morning the sun will struggle to burn through clouds.
(Do you remember her fiery ease in August?)
The sky hangs low to the frozen ground.
We walk through cloud forms.
(Are there constellations underneath?)
This ground is sacred
but is not holy alone.
This sphere is held
by an alchemy of perfection.
Moon and sun
the gravities of distance and magnitude
form fire and ice,
wave and tide.
Delight and wonder to the human eye
which is the only one to praise
such wonder with the tongue.
So, this day slowly glows to life.
The eye slowly opens in the sky.
Love peeks in on us
and the clouds catch blue fire.

A Trace of Us

Shall I make us Greek
because they recorded the names of people like us?
Patrocles and Achilles?
Alexander and Hephaestion?
Hadrian and Antinous?
Ignoring their slaves and empire?

Shall I invoke the names of the whispered?
The lovers that are clear to us
beyond burned letters and evasions?
David and Jonathan?
Whitman and Doyle?
Dali and Lorca?

Every choice will involve a fight with an enemy
who clings to the eraser in his hands.

Will there be a trace of us?
Does each sweet day bear the haunting line
that ages hence no one will remember
that men like us knew this kind of love?

Should I bow and give thanks
at our luck in having these days,
the minutes of truth and gentleness?

The Last Word of the Day is Love

The last word of the day is love.
Aside your soft warmth
I come to bed cold with the day's doubt.

You are afire deep in your dreams
purring the stories within you.
I move carefully but wake you.

Now at the surface of the pond,
I call out to you
before you descend again in dreams.

I give you the amulet of my love
that it watch over you in darkness
that it hold you in dreaming
to another daylight beside you.

TWO

Crickets & Yellow Dogs

They marched us into a multipurpose room,
a room named, in what I can only take
as a salute to our Roman forebears,
    the *cafetorium*.
Turn the chairs in one direction *voila* a cafeteria.
Turn the chairs in another direction *voila* an auditorium.

We filed in and sat in rows facing the stage.
They turned down the lights and showed us
a special Disney film meant to instruct us
in keeping ourselves pure.
Where my memory breaks I imagine Goofy sermonizing
on the finer points of daily hygiene.
Huey, Louie and Dewey,
illegitimate bastard ducklings of Daisy & Donald,
harmonizing about the food pyramid.
or at the very least a miming Pluto
washing behind his long floppy ears.

What I do remember involved a tuxedoed and
spat-footed cricket with top hat and cane who,
having guided Pinocchio through his perilous wooden journeys,
now appeared in a South Texas elementary school
with a warning to a room full of 2nd graders
to be careful what we touched.

    "I'm no fool, no sir-ee!
    I wanna live to be ninety-three!
    I play safe for you and me
    'Cause I'm no fool."

The warning was clear.
"Don't touch strange things."
"They might kill you," the cricket seemed to say.

It was many years before I learned
the life expectancy of crickets was 3 to 4 weeks.

Two years later they brought us in with the promise of popcorn
and when the room darkened
made us fall in love with an old yellow dog
who'd befriended a frontier family.

By the time the first reel had ended
and they turned on the lights to put on the next,
we were hard in love.
We were Texas barrio boys dreaming of having a dog,
just like that yellow dog
in that West Texas story

Then the second reel started
and the dog got bitten protecting the family from a wild boar.
And the boy who'd befriended the yellow dog
had to be a man,
had to shoot his yellow dog for having rabies.
And a room full of little macho fourth graders
tried not to blubber too loud in the dark cafetorium,
tried to wipe their tears away before the lights came back on.

"Don't touch strange things.
 They might kill you." The movie seemed to say.
"You might come down with something."
"The thing you love can turn on you,"
 Or even worse, you might have to kill the very thing you love.

What a horrible place the old West was.

Sleight of Hand Chicken Soup

When Tío Alberto came to visit
Papá sat him down in the kitchen.
And Alberto,
new to *los united státes*,
filled him in on the transition.

Papá asked if he wanted soup
and when Alberto said yes
Papá, not meaning a thing,
placed a bullion cube in a cup
and poured hot water from the tap.

But Tío Alberto didn't see any of that.
He was too busy talking about his new job
and how his girls were doing.
So when Papá handed him the cup he'd just stirred
Alberto sniffed at the rim and looked up in amazement.

¡Brigido!
This country is amazing!
They pipe chicken soup through the plumbing!

Such were the wonders of America.

The Sugars of Kindness

What did the woman say to her?

What did Ruthie say
to that woman who took the opportunity to call her a whore
in a language she figured Ruth too light-skinned to know?

She never told me what the woman said.
But it was bad enough to make the other women
in the check-out line blanch to silence.

No one joined her as she cussed my sister out.
Goddamning her I suspect,
maldiciendo her mother,
my mother,
because the line was long and she was in a hurry.

Ruth says she kept her cool,
no le subio el prú as we used to say,
as the women ahead came and went.

Finally the woman was before her,
and Ruth scanned her Velveeta, or Parkay,
or whatever the hell was in her basket,
all the time the woman clicking that poisonous tongue
and sending Ruth to the deeper circles of hell.

Finally Ruth took the woman's money,
gave the change and receipt
and in her flawless Spanish said,

"Muchísimas Gracias. Ha sido mi gran placer servirle hoy."
She thanked her with the sweetest sugars of kindness.

The woman turned white and started stuttering in two languages I suppose.

"No, no, no." Ruth smiled.

"You've said quite enough already."

English as a Second Irritating Language

Let her recite the hundred times this language
doesn't follow its own rules:

Nite.   N-I-T-E.
Night. N-I-G-H-T.
Knight. K-N-I-G-H-T.

And beware of the words that are so close to insult:
Bench.
Sheet.
Folk.

This tongue of exceptions
Which presented a minefield for my mother
Who only longed to be understood.

For Joel Who Held the Word for Me

After I came out to him,
he came to me,
and with tears in his eyes
removed the story from his body,
unwrapped it from the layers of memory.

The word.
The memory of the word.
The first time he'd heard of people like me.

He thinks he heard it before I was born.
But he was so young and the word sounded so odd
he said it "tickled his ears."

He was in church and Papá was in the pulpit
and he spoke the word
abominación.

Years later and a thousand miles away
he looked up at me,
my silent brother who sheltered me like a tree,
teaspoon tears running down his eyes,
he looked up to see if I remembered.

I had no memory.
And I had no doubt.

Somehow he carried it for me,
the thorn and the wound of the thorn.
He held it for me,
through all my years of wandering.

Father's Day for Gay Boys

One beside another — brothers
Seven diviners
of what lies beyond the truths we have uncovered.
One makes three, then four, then more
until we move beyond mere numbers.
There is thunder over the city tonight
and of the million hearts we may never see
here in the circle we make commitments
we push the limits of earthly loving.

Electricity visits again
and the black skies pulse with light —
currents of power by some capillary action.

Sons kiss their fathers.
Sons kiss their fathers to sleep
and the rose-eyed boy remembers himself again.

We are not the sons they ordered
with their patriotic dreaming.
We are not the sons they expected to come down the line.

But we unfold
beyond such kind paternal ignorance.
We unfold within the measure of our time.
And we make peace with the fathers inside of us.
And we give birth to a hidden, long-carried joy within.

Fe Esperanza y Caridad

In the picture she gingerly rests against the daffodil,
miraculous wonder of her adopted country's winter.

Her brothers smile behind her.
Tití delighted and Ignacio surprised
to have made it this far North in one lifetime.

Caruca, who bears the name of charity
smiles so delicately,
posed along my sister's flowerbed.
It is Spring in the picture
and my father and aunt are happy to have
their little brother beside them.

Ten years from now they will be happy
my father has survived a stroke and four months
of intensive care.

But now they are together again
and their children can never know
how far they have come
from *palmiches* and the back roads of Santa Clara.

In the background the sidewalk is broken,
and I am reminded of the mosaic floor they installed by hand
in the main house of the farm I have never seen.

She is gone now,
the daughter who grew to resemble her steadfast mother,
who always held court at an open table.
Ignacio still laughs to have befriended his strange circumstance
and Tití shades his eyes from the sun of his dreams.

I Have No Poems for You Now Texas

Everything's bigger with you
the bigger shame
the bigger loss
the nation's idiot albatross.

Charmless epitome of the national baby mind.
Tantrum little emperor.
Elector of buffoons.
Exiler of artists.
Kingmaker of rudeness.

How to make sense of your lost promises?
Your spoiled land and polluted waters?
Your stygian scholastic ignorance?
Your blind hooting pride from the end of all
lists of intelligence, well-being and infant mortality.

I have no poems for you now Texas,
save the ones that would surely lead me to your busy gallows
or to your brimming cup of hemlock
for leading your youth to the truth of you.

THREE

While the Audience Waits for the Poet to Finish Explaining the Poem He Has Yet to Read

If the poem must be unwrapped,
how much is gift,
and how much is pretty paper?

Gerald Early Can't See Latinos

He can't see Latinos.
He can't see Sammy Sosa.
And he can't see Pedro Martinez.

I don't even like baseball
but I can see them.

When Gerald Early writes 800 words in *Time* magazine
about how Jackie Robinson's legacy has withered away
and asks why there so few "black ball players today?"
but can't bring himself to mention all the dark-skinned Dominicans,
Cubans, Panamanians and Columbians,
I figure Gerald Early can't see Latinos.

But this is Gerald Early!
Esteemed professor of jazz, boxing and modern letters!
Biographer of Miles and Jack Johnson!
Writer on Race, Identity, and the Ambivalence of Assimilation!

If Gerald Early can't see Latinos,
You *know* something must be going on.
Like some perpetuation of a rule.
Perhaps we'll call it the rule of "Unforgivable Latinoness"
(To riff on Gerald Early's take on Jack Johnson),
The rule that reads that if you speak with an accent,
Especially a Spanish accent,
you're invisible in the African-American imagination.

Tell that to Julio Franco, Edgar Renteria, or José Contreras.
Tell that to Orlando Cabrera, Orlando Hernández,
or his brother Livan.

But someone else better tell them.
Because Gerald Early can't see Latinos.

Translating the Family Feud

"That's crazy!"
"That's silly!" he said.

I tried explaining how the Muslims, Christians and Jews have the same grandfather.

He stopped me every other sentence for the meaning of the words:
  "prophet"
  "messiah"
  "patriarch"
Which he would type into his handheld to find the translation in Cantonese.

I found myself having to explain it myself,
this story half told badly in Sunday Schools
placed before the funhouse mirror of single entendre.

"So, Muhammad recognized Jesus?"
"As a prophet" I told him, "not as the son of God."
"Where did the Muslims live after God promised
  Hagar and her child life and a nation of their own?"

I didn't have all the answers.
And it began to spin outward insanely.

"So, they're all related?"
"Yes."

"That's crazy."
"That's silly."

I realized the difficulty of translating stupidity.

Spitzer Linked to a Prostitution Ring

"Everyone always has a secret life" Kim says.

Spitzer. The good boy DA,
the anti-corruption crusader,
now found to have ordered in at the Mayflower.
A $4000 dollar tab
eight floors up from
where J. Edgar and Tolson
lunched in monotony for 20 years.

"But he was such a straight shooter" I say,
"No one saw any signs."

She says, "Those are the one I immediately suspect."
"Those are the ones I suspect."

Celibacy

The nipple that will not be touched
will not be sucked,
The fur that will not be stroked
will not be raked,
The flesh that will not be plied
will not be quaked,
The warmth that will not be shared
enfolded in the arms of another,
the sweat that will not be supped
in the middle of the night.

These reveal your god to be a waster of beauty
and a vanquisher of fire.

For Some Executors of Gay Writers

For the manuscript you kept locked up in a wall safe,
For the diaries you made sure would not be discovered,
For the letters from lovers you burned in the furnace,
For the measures you took to tear out their tongues,
For all of the ways you straightened the record,
For the zeal with which you smothered all knowledge,
For condemning the lovers to eternal silence,

May you see their faces in each mirror you gaze in.
May the names of their loved ones ring in your ears.
May you wake in the night to the sound of their fucking,
and be forced to lose sleep to all of their groans.
May the pages you hide catch fire from their smoldering,
till the wall safe explodes and consumes your house whole.
May you escape to find your charmed life in ruins.
May you call out in grief but hear nothing but silence.

On the Removal of Red

Every year, officials with the conservative Muslim kingdom's Commission for the Promotion of Virtue and Prevention of Vice clamp down on shops a few days before February 14, instructing them to remove red roses, red wrapping paper, gift boxes and teddy bears. On the eve of the holiday, they raid stores and seize symbols of love. CNN

Let us mark blood and love and danger with it.

Let us blush the cheeks of Raggedy Ann and Andy too with it,

Let us tinge flamingos with it,
flood the rose with it,
dress our jolly saints with it,
light our scandalous streets with it.

Let us mark blood and love and danger with it.

Let us signal stops with it,
warm our dashboard lights with it,
smear our pinko dupes with it,
wrap our chocolate hearts with it.

Let us mark blood and love and danger with it.

Let us burn our Dylan Thomas hearts with it,
kindle fires of justice with it,
scald the thought police with it,
spank the bottoms of the silly law with it.

Let us mark blood and love and danger with it.

FOUR

The Cold Rush of Comparisons

The news broke in the *New York Times*
that by the year 2032
with the help of computers and search engines
all the metaphors of poets would be exhausted.

The ad agencies, smelling a fresh well,
began to trademark the remaining ones.
Jell-O commercials, after all, do not write themselves.

The language poets remained unfazed.
Metaphors floated by them like cows in Calcutta.

In 2020, with the deadline fast approaching,
The Supreme Court declared all metaphor and simile
the final frontier.
And then the gold rush began in earnest.

When the ases and likes had been pinned down
they went trolling for others.

Weyerhauser speculated in Kilmer's trees
while Monsanto bought up Erica Jong's tomatoes
and even Orlovsky's smiling vegetables.
3M applied and won the patents to Pope and Mallarmé,
while FedEx bought the use of all poems on speed and
punctuality.

We Learn How Greed Grows

Just enough for a sprinkle,
enough for a tart,
for a pie,
two pies,
enough for all winter.

The hand fills,
the cup fills,
then the lip of the bucket,
till we reach the limits of containment.

By the second hour,
we have begun engineering the perfect berry picker,
long arms,
hunched low to the ground,
with eyes attuned to the ruby hues
and the invisible blues.

The berries taunt us to be picked.
"We are the sun itself!" they seem to say.
"Grab us all to remind you in the winter cold ahead."

And the birds seem grossly negligent to ignore
such extravagant clinging.

The Nature of His Knowing

He knows somehow
the exact moment I am coming to bed.
There is never a false alarm on his part.
Before I rise from the chair
he leaves my side of the bed
and moves to the floor to round himself in place.

Some nights I call him back to bed
to lie beside me,
to touch fur,
to hear his soft animal breathing.

This night I enter in darkness
and make my way to his bed.
I kneel and give thanks to this body of motion,
this creature of hair and bone.
I stroke his ears and whisper a blessing
for the nature of his knowing,
for the gifts he freely gives.

Constellations of Delight

This morning you are a blessing on four legs,
nose greeting the snow before you
tail brushing the snow behind you
your form electric in the falling snow.

What to make of this,
the world gone ecstatic white?
What to make of this,
dog with all legs four for happiness?
Black face with snowy constellations of delight?

After a while, you pleaded to come inside
with liquid brown eyes of anticipation.

In the winter of warring dread
we are all this dog wanting
to come in from the cold.

In Which the Poet Savors the Chicken Soup Brought to Him at the Very Hour of His Need

The broth must taste of chicken,
the very feather and pluck,
that when tasted leaves you imagining
the very bird inside you clucks.

In the swim of this pure chickenness
flits the green of parsley or celery,
not so firm as to cast the mind infirmed beyond
the healing chicken.

All is chicken.
All must be chicken for the flu-sick mind.

How did he pack a flock of chickens into this bowl?
He imagines a Shriner's convention in the convention hall
of his head where the roosters wear fezzes and ride around
in tiny little cars of down.

Once nourished, the recuperating
dreams his chicken dreams,
pecks the dirt beyond all reason,
hears a reassuring cluck between his ears.

Ode to the Black Nationalist Pharaoh Head of Georgia Avenue

Oh how we have need of you
Black Nationalist Pharaoh Head of Georgia Avenue.

How we have need of your proud scowl gazing down
on Harvard Street as we make our way home each day.

Here among European diasporic architecture,
colonial, deco, craftsman, rowhouse,
you lorded over the mild and the meek,
handsome in your headdress, reminding your people
of their roots in a land of historic geometries.

No scepter or servants,
just that head jutting out
from the Black Nationalist bookshop
where my friend once entered,
and being told it was only for blacks,
asked, "How do you know that I'm not?"

Oh Black Nationalist Pharaoh Head of Georgia Avenue,
who took you down when they closed up the bookshop?
Where did they cart you to, Black Nationalist Pharaoh Head?
What avenues do you gaze down upon now?
What message do you impart to the hungering crowds?

I imagine you now in Africa,
in the Kush, rubbing elbows with other Pharaoh heads,
gazing upon your pyramids again.

The empty wall here calls for you.
For we still have need of you
Black Nationalist Pharaoh Head of Georgia Avenue.
Your gaze is still needed.

Sterling On 12th Street

For Sterling Brown and Brookland

If Sterling were alive I imagine him walking down 12th street.
or running into him at the hardware store
or eating breakfast with Daisy at Murry & Paul's.

I am sure I'd see Dutch being greeted by name at the post office
while he waited in line for the friendly postal clerk
you know the one,
in the last window with the only smiling face?

But I am just imagining this.
I never knew him or his steps in this place.
But I can imagine.
We can imagine what it means to live in a place with history.
We can remember even what we have never known.

When the new market opens on 12th street.
Let us remember the old Co-op that struggled
    and gave people fresh produce while it struggled.
Let us remember the Safeway that stood there before that.
Let us remember the houses that gave way for the Safeway.
Let us remember the hillside that gave way for the houses.
Let us remember the woods that Ann Brooks spied
    from the back window of the mansion.
    when all the hills were green with trees.

About the Author

Dan Vera's poetry has appeared in *Beltway Poetry Quarterly, Delaware Poetry Review, Konch,* the anthologies *DC Poets Against the War* and *Dog Blessings,* and featured on Pacifica Radio.

A regular reader throughout the Washington, DC area, Dan also curates two reading series in the city and has been known to lead walking tours on the literary history of some of the city's neighborhoods.

This is his first published collection of poetry.

For more about Dan visit
www.danvera.com

On Type

Cheltenham, used here for the text of poems, is an old style serif typeface designed by the neo-gothic and art-deco architect Bertram Grosvenor Goodhue and Ingalls Kimball in 1896 for use by the Cheltenham Press. Cheltenham is not based on a single historical model, but shows influences of the Arts and Crafts Movement. It reached wide popularity through the efforts of the famous type designer Morris Fuller Benton.

In 1933 Morris Fuller Benton designed **Eagle Bold** for Franklin Delano Roosevelt's National Recovery Administration. Used in the famous "blue eagle" posters of the New Deal, the type became the symbol of American recovery and was modernized in the 1990s. Jonathan Corum designed the light weight which is used here for titles and ancillary information.

About
BEOTHUK BOOKS

Beothuk Books takes its name from the aboriginal people of Newfoundland, the Beothuk. During European colonization, the Beothuk refused to ally themselves with the French, English or other Native American tribes and remained isolated. They were subsequently devastated by the effects of that colonization: other tribes routinely raided their villages, settlers forced them into Newfoundland's inhospitable interior, and European diseases were rampant and deadly. By the mid-1800's, the Beothuk were extinct.
The Beothuk language, itself unrelated to other Native American language groups, now survives as a few hundred vocabulary words.
If language is the habitat of a people's culture, then poetry is both a preserver of that habitat and a guide through it. Poetry points out and embodies language's fragilities and strengths, its nuances, and its vibrant ecosystem. Poetry reifies the language of the tribe. In choosing the name of a gone language, Beothuk Books hopes to remind us of and honor that connection. - Michael Gushue

For more information visit
www.beothukbooks.com

www.ingramcontent.com/pod-product-compliance
Ingram Content Group UK Ltd.
Pitfield, Milton Keynes, MK11 3LW, UK
UKHW041959230426
12048UKWH00008B/418

9 780615 253710